# LIVERPOOL CATHEDRAL

## A Welcome from the Dean

Welcome to Liverpool Cathedral, one of the great buildings of Western Europe.

The cathedral stands above the city, reminding all who see it as they go about their business of the 'things of God'. It reminds people of the call to worship, the need to consider the values which shape our culture, which inform and enrich our lives and which govern our conduct in the place where we work or play, and our relationships with those who are close to us.

During the year hundreds of thousands of people come here – some as visitors to marvel at the artistry and architecture, some to join in great civic or national occasions, some to sit quietly in the presence of God and in silence reflect on the pain and the joy of living.

For my part as Dean I give God thanks for the privilege of being here and for the team of men, women and children who help to make this such a special place.

Of one thing I am certain; those who enter this cathedral are changed by the experience and join in giving thanks to God for the vision and generosity of our founders and benefactors who brought it into being.

To build one of the great buildings of the century is any architect's dream. To be given the chance to design a cathedral as one's first real commission is an unbelievable fantasy. But then Liverpool is a place where artistic dreams come true.

When the new diocese of Liverpool was formed in 1890 out of the ancient diocese of Chester, the city was one of the most significant in Britain outside London, and a centre for trade and emigration, famous around the world. Liverpool's citizens welcomed the chance to celebrate this new stage in their history and to demonstrate the forward-looking confidence of a community based not just on prosperity, but also on its faith.

The first Bishop of Liverpool, Bishop Ryle, used St Peter's Church as his cathedral but it was not really suitable to transform into a Mother Church for the diocese. Bishop Chavasse, the second Bishop, had other ideas. A committee was formed with his encouragement and, at a meeting chaired by the Earl of Derby in 1901, the decision was taken to build a cathedral which would express the aspirations and commitment of the city. A panel considered the suggestions of a short list of five architects and chose the winning design, by Giles Gilbert Scott. In some ways they surprised even themselves by their decision. Not only had they chosen the work of a young man of 22 who had hardly finished his training, he was also a Roman Catholic. In the atmosphere that existed between the churches at the time this was a sensitive decision.

*RIGHT: The Very Revd. F.W. Dwelly was first Dean of Liverpool. He had devised the service for the consecration of the cathedral in 1924 and was appointed Dean when the Chapter was founded in 1931. He was responsible for developing many of the distinctive elements of the cathedral ceremonial including the design of its robes and furnishings. In particular he established the Cross Guild, a fellowship for former choristers, to take a formal part in processions and worship.* ⑱

In spite of this they decided to proceed, but insisted that the young architect should work with one of the assessors, G.F. Bodley RA, who was established in the profession.

Scott found this relationship quite difficult and soon considered abandoning the project. But Bodley died in 1907, leaving the younger architect to forge ahead with what was to be his life's most important work – one of the great buildings of the 20th century.

ABOVE: HM King George and Queen Mary leave the cathedral after the Service of Consecration on 19 July 1924. The Lady Chapel and east end are complete but work on the tower has not yet begun.

ABOVE: *A memorial to the Earl of Derby, whose family have lived on the outskirts of Liverpool for many years. It was designed by Scott and incorporates the cathedral as a slightly uncomfortable support for his pillow. There is also a little mouse peeping out from under the cushion which children love to find. Over the years small hands have burnished its nose to a high polish!*

## SIR GILES GILBERT SCOTT

*Born 1880. Died 1960.*

He obtained the commission in 1903. Major buildings: Battersea Power Station, Cambridge University Library, Ampleforth Abbey, Yorkshire.

His smallest building is the famous red telephone box; there is one in the cathedral – pictured right. ㉒

His grandfather was Sir George Gilbert Scott, responsible for St Pancras Station, the Albert Memorial and much restoration of cathedrals.

3

To the Glory of God
This foundation stone was laid by
King Edward the Seventh
on the 19th day of July 1904

The foundation stone, which weighs four tons, is the largest stone in the building. It contains mementos of the period – copies of local and national papers (the Liverpool Mercury, Courier, Post and The Times), a list of the General Committee, a copy of the Cathedral Act of Parliament, a special edition of the Cathedral Committee's Handbook and the form of service used at the ceremony. **18**

*MAIN PICTURE: As the cathedral grew, it came to dominate the streets of houses which lay on its southern flank. This area was seriously damaged by bombing in the Second World War; the houses were eventually demolished, to be replaced in recent years by a modern development for the cathedral.*

*BELOW: Men who worked on the construction needed a good head for heights. The stones were cut to shape in the masons' yard on the ground and then hoisted up on to the scaffold for the fixer masons to bed them into position.*

The great west window is a magnificent example of work by Carl Edwards, whose stained glass enriches many churches and cathedrals. It was given by Sir Alan and Lady Tod and expresses the Benedicite, *a hymn of praise to God by all creation. Within its 1,486 square metres (16,000 square feet) can be found many aspects of the natural world, rainbows, beasts of the fields, sun and moon – including a night view of the Mersey dominated by the Liver building.* ❶

RIGHT: *For many of the craftsmen who helped to build the cathedral it was their whole career. At its peak the workforce was 240 strong. Many men began as apprentices and worked there for the rest of their lives. It would be hard to recruit such a large group of craftsmen today.*

**FACT FILE**

| | | |
|---|---|---|
| Length | 201 metres | (660 feet) |
| Height of tower | 101 metres | (331 feet) |
| Height of central space | 53 metres | (175 feet) |
| Width of central space | 22 metres | (73 feet) |
| Width of transepts | 61 metres | (199 feet) |

Construction:    local sandstone with brick and concrete structural elements

Floor:    Hopton Wood stone (a decorative limestone originating in Derbyshire)

Most people who enter the cathedral from the west end find the prospect of its sweeping piers, soaring arches, its high vaulted roof and towering windows an awesome sight. It is probably the final manifestation in Britain of the Gothic style of cathedral construction which was at its peak 700 years ago. But Sir Giles Gilbert Scott also exploited modern techniques and

LEFT: *Windows in the nave commemorate those whose lives have contributed to the richness of the worship of the whole church, and the beauty which surrounds that worship. Theologians, composers, clergy and scholars, hymnwriters and laymen are all honoured. This detail from the layman's window depicts tradesmen and craftsmen who worked on the building.* ㉓

material in its construction to stretch traditional style to new and exciting proportions.

The cathedral was built from local sandstone over a period of 74 years: first the Lady Chapel, followed by the sanctuary, choir and eastern transepts. Then came the vast central space with the tower and the western transepts which were completed during the Second World War. Finally the nave and the west end were finished, although not incorporating Scott's plan for an elaborate porch. Sir Giles died in 1960 and it was his colleague Frederick Thomas who saw the project through with the assistance of Roger A. Pinkney. The cathedral was finally dedicated in 1978 in the presence of HM Queen Elizabeth II.

Liverpool Cathedral is a building of superlatives. It is the largest Anglican cathedral in the country and at the time of its dedication was among the five largest in the world, of which St Peter's in Rome remains pre-eminent.

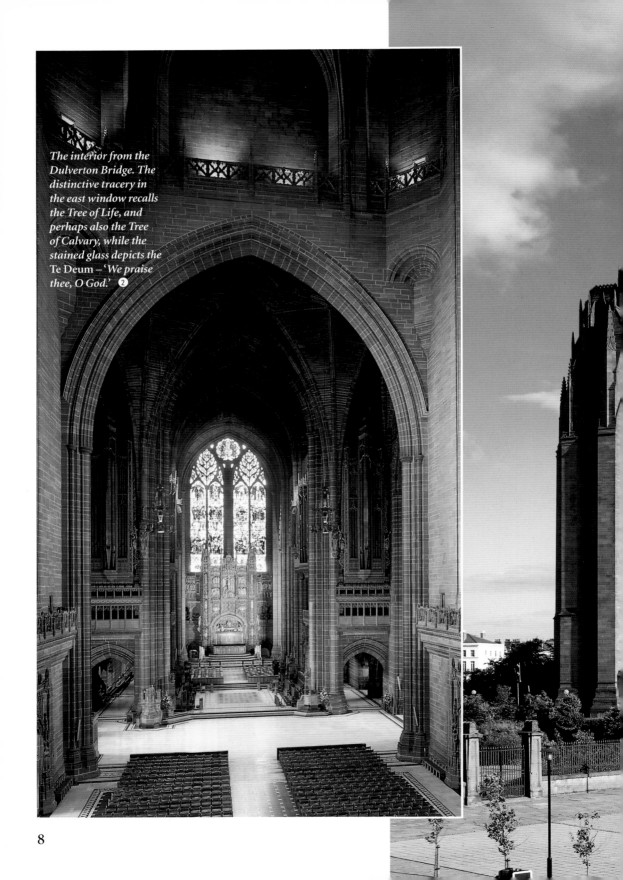

The interior from the Dulverton Bridge. The distinctive tracery in the east window recalls the Tree of Life, and perhaps also the Tree of Calvary, while the stained glass depicts the Te Deum – 'We praise thee, O God.' ❷

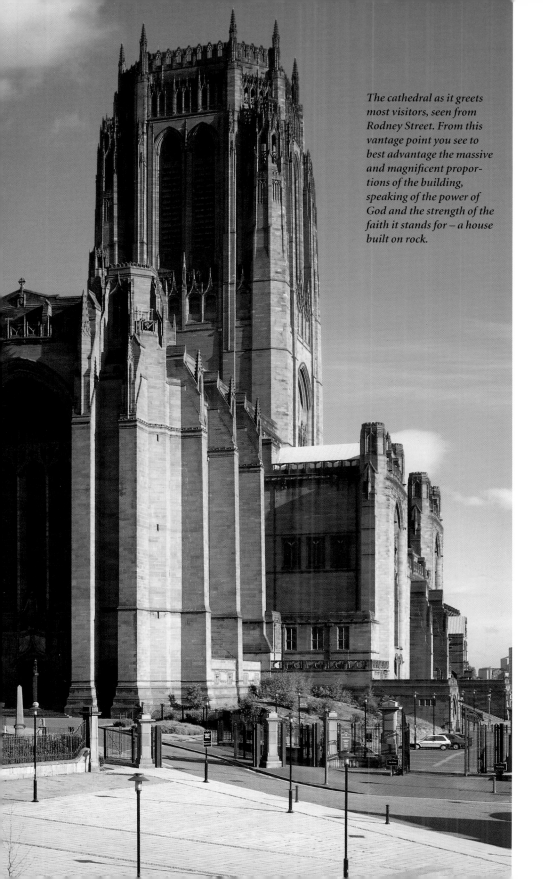

*The cathedral as it greets most visitors, seen from Rodney Street. From this vantage point you see to best advantage the massive and magnificent proportions of the building, speaking of the power of God and the strength of the faith it stands for – a house built on rock.*

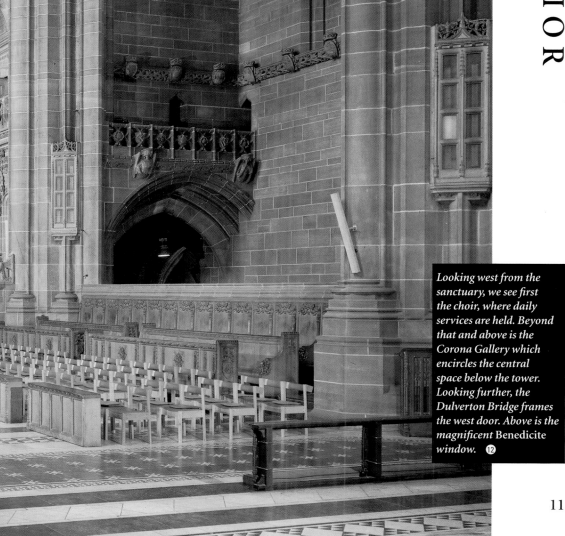

*Looking west from the sanctuary, we see first the choir, where daily services are held. Beyond that and above is the Corona Gallery which encircles the central space below the tower. Looking further, the Dulverton Bridge frames the west door. Above is the magnificent Benedicite window.* **12**

11

The floor plan of the cathedral is in the shape of a double-armed cross. This unusual configuration has given rise to the cathedral emblem which is used in various ways in the life of the cathedral, on the vergers' maces, on various robes and badges and as a general 'logo'.

The arms of the crosses are the transepts. At the west end of the cathedral the south transept is called the baptistry, as it accommodates the large ceremonial font. The north-west transept houses the cathedral SPCK shop, dominated by the billowing sails of the 'Spirit of Liverpool'. This aerial sculpture, subtly changing colour each hour, was designed by the present cathedral architect, Keith Scott.

The window in the baptistry, together with the grand oak and gilt housing for the font, emphasizes the importance of baptism as the rite which marks

*The Visitor Centre. Looking across the north-west transept, one sees the 'Spirit of Liverpool' which connects the cathedral to the seafaring traditions of the city. Millions sailed from the port to seek fortune in the new colonies across the Atlantic and on the other side of the world.* ③

BELOW: *The cathedral's refectory has been recommended for four consecutive years by Egon Ronay. It was developed in the Welsford Porch to benefit visitors and regular patrons in search of light meals and refreshments.* ⑤

the beginning of the Christian life. One of the instructions which Jesus gave to his followers was to 'baptize people everywhere in the name of God – Father, Son and Holy Spirit'.

In baptism, water is used to symbolize cleansing, also to symbolize life. The motif on the floor around the font depicts the sea, with fish swimming around, linking us with the idea of the Israelites passing to their new life through the waters of the Red Sea from the slavery of Egypt.

The marble font itself has twelve sides, each carved with a representation of one of the Apostles, reminding us that children or adults who are baptized in it today are embracing the same Christian faith which was preached 2000 years ago.

LEFT: *The twelve-sided font is carved from a block of 'lunel rubane', a warm-coloured marble from France. On each of its faces is a figure representing one of the Apostles. Dominating the south-west transept is the highly decorated baldachino (*TOP*), the font's great oak cover which towers up to over 12 metres (39 feet).* ㉑

The Vestey tower, so called because of the enormous generosity of the family in supporting its construction, is one of the dominating features of the Liverpool skyline. It is wonderfully exciting to see it floodlit against the night sky, wreathed in low cloud, or standing proud in the sunlight, reaching 101 metres (331 feet) into the sky.

In the original design for the cathedral there were to be two towers of 80 metres (260 ft); this was changed by Scott in 1910 to a single tower 85 metres (280 ft) high. In 1924 he raised the height even further and fined down its bulk. The final design is complex, with a carefully calculated taper and wonderful detail on the pinnacles and turrets, rarely noticed by the casual observer.

The tower houses the ringing chamber and belfry which itself is distinctive, incorporating the highest and heaviest ringing peal in the world. Considerable ingenuity and extensive use of modern materials were used in the construction of the whole to ensure that the bells can safely be rung. They witness to the population at large that the worship of the cathedral is taking place, or that events of significance have occurred. The largest bell, Great George, weighs nearly 14.75 tons, and is tolled only for special occasions in the life of the cathedral or the community, such as the death of a monarch, or the death of a Dean or Bishop.

*BELOW: A bell is hoisted up to the belfry through a circular hole in the ceiling of the central space. In the nave, the 14-ton Great George waits his turn.* ④

*RIGHT: The circular cast concrete frame which holds the 14 bells is an ingenious design peculiar to the cathedral. This allows a straight fall for the bell ropes to the ringing chamber below. The bells and their mountings need to be regularly inspected and maintained if they are to stand up to the rigours of peals lasting up to two hours.* ㉒

BELOW: *The view from the tower is spectacular – across the city and Liverpool Bay. It is also possible to see the Welsh hills and, sometimes, Blackpool Tower and the Lake District. The tower is regularly open to the public, involving a ride in two separate lifts and a climb of 108 steps up the inside of the tower which affords an exciting view of the bell chamber.* (22)

LEFT: *The model of Scott's original design with twin towers has been meticulously restored to show how the concept changed while building progressed.* (18)

ABOVE: **The Welcoming Christ** *by Dame Elisabeth Frink.*
*Cast in bronze, it stands nearly 5 metres (16 feet) high and*
*weighs over half a ton. It looks out over the city expressing*
*the concern of Christ and his Church for all people.* ①

Liverpool Cathedral is itself a work of art, an expression of beauty and spirituality in stone and wood. When you stand beneath the Dulverton Bridge looking towards the high altar, it is hard not to be moved by the graceful proportions of the arches and pillars, by the colour and elegance of the stained-glass windows and the gilded magnificence of the reredos – the screen behind the altar.

But the cathedral is also the setting for works of art. There are figures sculpted in bronze, stone and wood – memorials, biblical figures, some an expression of spiritual ideals or aspects of worship. Religious art enriches the teaching of the church and inspires the faith of believers.

LEFT: The Good Samaritan *by Adrian Wiszniewski, who was brought up as a Roman Catholic in a Polish family which had settled in Glasgow. His painting is deeply symbolic. The robber's victim he identifies with Christ – himself a victim at his crucifixion – stripped and wounded. The sky is black and the time is 3.00 pm, the traditional hour of Jesus' death. Business-men and passers-by ignore the victim. Only the Good Samaritan – strikingly portrayed as a woman – holds out a cup of water.* ⑳

Looking across the city from above the great west door stands *The Welcoming Christ*, the last work of Dame Elisabeth Frink CH, dedicated on Easter Day 1994, shortly before the sculptor's death.

The south-west triforium houses the Elizabeth Hoare Gallery, a unique collection of ecclesiastical embroidery.

There are paintings, too, the most important of which are the two pairs of paintings based on parables, specially commissioned for Liverpool Cathedral and given by the Jerusalem Trust. One pair, by Christopher Le Brun, hangs in the choir stalls evoking the parables of the Good Samaritan and the Prodigal Son. In the central space we find the striking work of Adrian Wiszniewski interpreting in a

ABOVE: *A maquette (or sculptor's model) of Dame Elisabeth Frink's* The Welcoming Christ, *placed at the east end of the south choir aisle as a focus for prayer and reflection.* ⑭

contemporary idiom the House built on Rock and the Good Samaritan.

Such works of art are a form of communication which invite a response from those who experience them, which inspire a mood, or offer a creative moment of reflection on the world in which we live.

BELOW: *Christopher Le Brun's painting, based on the parable of the Prodigal Son, was given to the cathedral by the Jerusalem Trust. It depicts the moment of return, with the son being greeted in joy by his father and mother and the family pet dog. At the right, the elder brother lurks in the bushes, nursing his jealousy.* ⑩

One of the artistic treasures of the Church of England is the cathedral tradition of choral worship. Liverpool does not have a choir school but still manages to recruit committed and gifted singers, men and boys, who regularly sing at services. Their repertoire includes works by all the major composers of church music. Styles range from formal classical settings of the Mass to Professor Ian Tracey's arrangement of 'You'll never walk alone' which was sung at the memorial service after the Hillsborough football disaster.

An important part of this tradition of church music involves the use of organ as accompaniment and also as a solo instrument to thrill and delight congregations with voluntaries before and after services and within the liturgy.

The main organ is itself a remarkable instrument. Installed by Henry Willis & Sons between 1923 and 1926, it was overhauled and modernized in the late fifties. In 1977 there was a further overhaul by Harrison & Harrison of Durham. It is the largest organ in the UK and one of the largest in the world. It plays a fitting part in the musical life of the cathedral which boasts a full programme of recitals drawing visitors from many miles around.

*RIGHT: The organist perches in a gallery above the choir. The design of the organ casing is an integrated part of the whole concept adding to the majestic effect. The layout of the main console is exactly replicated in a mobile console on the floor of the cathedral (see inset). This is used mainly for recitals, concerts and occasionally for services in the central space.* ⑨

## ORGAN FACT FILE

Five manuals plus pedal board with electric action.

Two consoles each with 145 speaking stops and 38 couplers.

9,704 pipes ranging in size from 10-metre (32-foot) pedal stops to 2-centimetre (3/4-inch) Spitzflote on the choir organ.

Three electric powered rotary blowers – total output 48 h.p.

Two organ chambers and four swell boxes.

*The choir at evensong. None of the members is full time. Boys are drawn from a number of local schools. Men have day jobs and among them are teachers, accountants, civil servants, a draughts-man and an organ builder.*

*BELOW:* Professor Ian Tracey at the console of the organ. From the first, there has been a succession of musicians associated with the cathedral who have contributed to the musical life of the city and the country. As well as providing the musical expertise for the religious life of the cathedral, the organist and his assistants offer help with performance and teaching to a variety of groups and individuals.

After the laying of the foundation stone in 1904, the first part of the cathedral to be completed was the Lady Chapel. It is at the east end of the building, reached by a staircase from a gallery opening out of the south choir aisle. Here can be seen the main fruits of the period of cooperation between Scott and Bodley; especially notable is the rather more elaborate style, the distinctive reredos above and behind the altar and the ornate carving running around the chapel walls of the Gospel text 'God so loved the world …'.

The Lady Chapel is a little like a parish church attached to the cathedral, complete with its own organ and entrance. Aesthetically and practically, though, it remains an important part of the whole cathedral. After its completion in 1910, services were held here until the first part of the main cathedral was consecrated in 1924. Separate access to the Lady Chapel is through the children's porch to the Queen's Walk which runs beside the cathedral.

The stained-glass windows in the Lady Chapel depict women of significance from the Bible and from different periods of church history. Many of the original windows were badly damaged by bombs during the Second World War and had to be reworked.

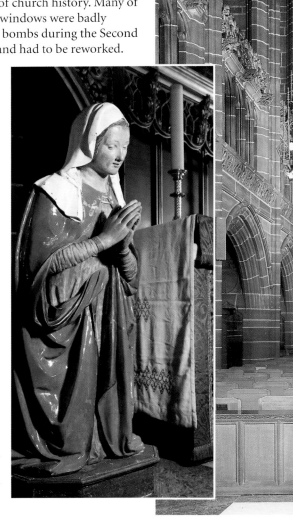

*BELOW: Detail from a window on the staircase leading down to the Lady Chapel from the south choir aisle. It celebrates a number of important women, some of them local like Kitty Wilkinson and Agnes Jones who worked for poor people in Liverpool. Louisa Stewart, pictured here, was martyred in China while serving with the Church Missionary Society. In July 1995 her granddaughter, great-granddaughter and two great-great-grandchildren were joined by present supporters of CMS to mark the centenary of her martyrdom.* ⑯

*RIGHT: This charming statue of the Virgin Mary can be found in the Lady Chapel. It is by Giovanni della Robbia, an Italian sculptor of the 15th century, and is an important example of his work. He used porcelain glazes as well as normal pigmentation. There is another example of della Robbia's work in Portsmouth Cathedral.* ⑮

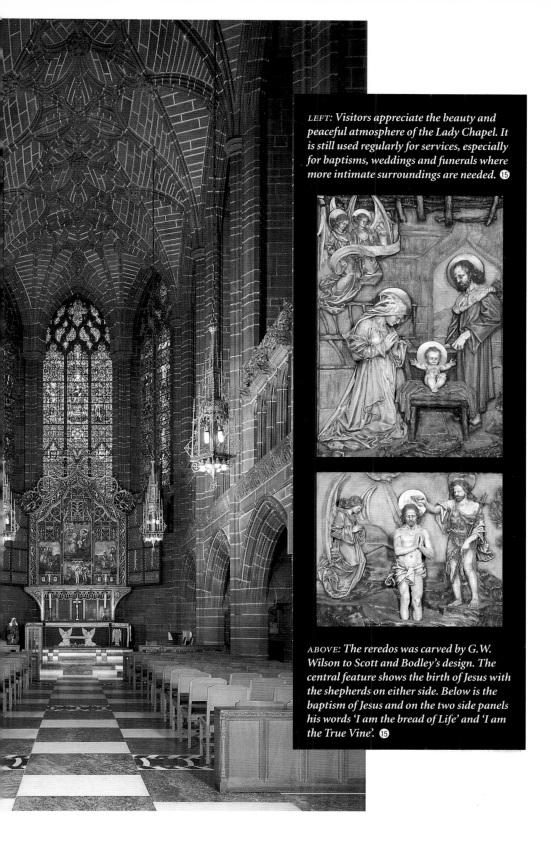

LEFT: *Visitors appreciate the beauty and peaceful atmosphere of the Lady Chapel. It is still used regularly for services, especially for baptisms, weddings and funerals where more intimate surroundings are needed.* **15**

ABOVE: *The reredos was carved by G.W. Wilson to Scott and Bodley's design. The central feature shows the birth of Jesus with the shepherds on either side. Below is the baptism of Jesus and on the two side panels his words 'I am the bread of Life' and 'I am the True Vine'.* **15**

*RIGHT: A soldier honours the memory of those who fought in his regiment before him. The King's Own Liverpool Regiment is one of several such units which make a regular pilgrimage to the cathedral to pay their respects and to remember their tradition of service.* ⑥

*RIGHT: Football fans gathered in the cathedral with their insignia to remember Bob Paisley, former manager of Liverpool F.C.*

*LEFT: The bell of the warship HMS Liverpool is a strong symbol of the close ties between the city and the sea. Young visitors often ring it to experience the sound of the echo sustained by the building.* ⑦

A cathedral is a church for the whole community, a sanctuary for its worship and a shrine where people can commemorate and honour their ancestors and heroes. The north-west transept is the main focus within the cathedral to remember the two World Wars, both of which took place during the course of its building. Here we find military colours and standards, service emblems and, most specially, a record of the names of the fallen relating to all three services. The main Book of Remembrance records the 40,000 servicemen of Liverpool who died in the First World War. It is a magnificent volume, illuminated by George Scruby and signed by King George V.

One of the major annual events is the remembrance of the Battle of the Atlantic. This long and bitter campaign of the Second World War claimed the lives of many seamen in the struggle to keep vital supplies crossing the Atlantic from North America to the Allies in Europe. The bell of HMS

*ABOVE: Bishop Chavasse is commemorated on the rear of the Bishop's throne, which is the most important seat in the cathedral. He was the second Bishop of Liverpool, from 1900 to 1923. The memorial, which was designed by Scott, depicts the Bishop at prayer, supported by a cathedral which was then only partly built.* ⑰

*Liverpool* hanging at the entrance to the transept emphasizes the cathedral's close naval links.

Each month soldiers from the King's Own Liverpool Regiment attend Evensong to commemorate their former colleagues as they turn a leaf in their Book of Remembrance. The Burma Star Association also has a memorial here.

In the Memorial Chapel also is a bust which honours Captain Noel Chavasse, the only member of the armed forces to be awarded the Victoria Cross twice in the First World War. It is fitting that he should be remembered in the cathedral which his father, Bishop Francis James Chavasse, second Bishop of Liverpool, did so much to serve. Bishop Chavasse is buried in the precincts and honoured in a memorial behind the Bishop's throne.

M ost ancient cathedrals are divided by a screen between the main congregational nave and the choir. Part of the dramatic impact of Liverpool is that there is no barrier to block the view from the west end right through to the sanctuary. The gilded reredos behind and above the high altar dominates the whole building with its emphatic reminder of the central tenets of the Christian faith – the incarnation, the crucifixion and the resurrection. Also, just above the altar, the focus of Eucharistic worship, is a representation of the Last Supper. The carving, largely the work of Walter Gilbert and L. Weingarten, is integrated structurally into the east wall, leading the eye up to the great east window which takes for its theme one of the great hymns of praise used in morning prayer – the *Te Deum*.

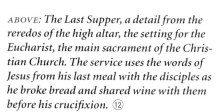

ABOVE: *The Last Supper, a detail from the reredos of the high altar, the setting for the Eucharist, the main sacrament of the Christian Church. The service uses the words of Jesus from his last meal with the disciples as he broke bread and shared wine with them before his crucifixion.* ⑫

*The high altar is the physical focus of the cathedral and also of its worship. With the east window it dominates the whole cathedral reminding us of the importance to the Christian faith of the crucifixion and the resurrection.*

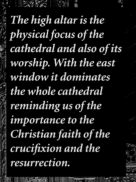

ABOVE: *From the Corona Gallery, we see the meticulous attention to detail in the design of the high altar. The creative use of coloured marble in the floor emphasizes the different areas of the cathedral.* ④

At the highest point of the window is Christ in Majesty, reminding us all that the whole building is dedicated to the resurrected Christ.

Close to the sanctuary on the south side of the choir is the Bishop's throne. It is the fact that the Bishop has his seat in this building – in Greek the word is *kathedra* – that gives the cathedral its title. In the floor of the chancel in front of the throne is a mosaic representation of the arms of the Diocese of Liverpool, which can be seen on the back cover of this guide.

LEFT: *The communion rail, marking the division between the choir and the sanctuary, is supported by ten exquisitely cast figures, each representing one of the ten commandments. This one recalls number six – thou shalt not commit adultery.* ⑫

25

From the glory of its Gothic grandeur to the design of its most delicate details, the building of the cathedral has been intended to provide an arena for public worship and private prayer. At least twice each day services of worship are held, sometimes with great musical magnificence, sometimes in stark simplicity. The scriptures are read and prayers are said for the work of the church and the needs of the world. Throughout the church's year there are special services which mark the passing seasons with popular celebrations in words and music.

Times of triumph and rejoicing for the city, like the ending of war and the coronation of the monarch, have been celebrated with appropriate ceremony. So too have times been marked of tragedy and sorrow, drawing together all elements of the community to share their common concern.

As the Mother Church for the diocese, the cathedral is host to services which draw together members of parishes from many miles apart to witness the ordination of their clergy, or to welcome new members of their community at confirmation.

In recent years a new dimension has entered the life of the cathedral, as it is not just used for Anglican worship. The Methodist Chairman held his inaugural service here, and a variety of other occasions have found great congregations from many parts of the Christian family united in prayer and praise, in celebration or common concern. There can have been few more evocative moments than the visit of His Holiness the Pope in 1982 with the first great Hope Street procession between the two cathedrals.

BELOW: *The octagonal Chapter House was built with donations from members of local lodges of Freemasons. Rarely used for formal meetings, it is regularly the venue for small midweek services.* ⑬

TOP: *The cathedral is thronged with worshippers attending the annual ceremony for the blessing of the tree, one of several popular services around the Christmas season.*

ABOVE: *The cathedral in party mood as church members from the whole diocese bid goodbye to the former Suffragan Bishop of Warrington, Bishop Michael Henshall.*

RIGHT: *The Chapel of the Holy Spirit is a special place for quiet prayer and meditation. Recently an aumbry has been installed where the Blessed Sacrament is reserved. The reredos portrays Jesus in prayer overlooking the Sea of Galilee. Sir Giles Gilbert Scott's design was carried out by William Gough.* ⑧

The Cathedral Church of Christ in Liverpool is indeed a great home for the whole Christian family. It has often resounded with the words of the Liverpool Blessing, pronounced by leaders from the Roman Catholic, Anglican and Free Churches:

> **God bless Liverpool and**
> **make her people**
> **strong in faith,**
> **steadfast in hope**
> **and generous in charity**
> **through Jesus Christ our Lord.**
> *Amen.*

*Liverpool Cathedral stands as a landmark over much of the city. It dominates the skyline with a sense of confidence and security. This is particularly striking when it is floodlit against the night sky.*